To Jonathan and Amanda, my favorite tree people —M.S.

For Mom, my own oak tree, who taught me to love the roots and the worms —J.P.

Many, many thanks to Jonathan Chesler, Four Springs Landscape & Garden, LLC, and Amanda Locke, Regional Forester at NYCDEP, for their scrupulous input, and to Gerri Griswold, Director of Administration and Development, White Memorial Conservation Center, for her expertise about bats.

Millbrook Press™
An imprint of Lerner Publishing Group, Inc.
241 First Avenue North
Minneapolis, MN 55401 USA

For reading levels and more information, look up this title at www.lernerbooks.com.

Designed by Athena Currier.
Main body text set in ITC Franklin Gothic Std. Typeface provided by Adobe Systems.
The artwork for this book was painted in gouache & colored pencil.

Library of Congress Cataloging-in-Publication Data

The Cataloging-in-Publication Data for *Whose Tree Is This?: Poems About the Mighty Oak and Its Companions* is on file at the Library of Congress.
ISBN 979-8-7656-7083-5 (lib. bdg.)
ISBN 979-8-7656-9982-9 (epub)

Manufactured in Guang Dong, China, by Dream Colour Printing
1-1012841-54102-7/11/2025

Whose Tree Is This?

Poems About the Mighty Oak and Its Companions

written by Marilyn Singer
illustrated by Julian Plum

Millbrook Press/Minneapolis

Whose Tree Is This?

Whose tree is this?
Reaching high, spreading wide,
this oak, so gracious, so spacious,
giving gifts throughout the year.
Acorns for eating, tree crooks for nests,
leaves that shelter many guests.

Whose tree is this?
Growing strong, living long,
this oak, inviting, delighting
visitors both large and small,
travelers from far and near:
Come, spend some time right here.

Caterpillar

This is my tree.
I hatched in a batch
this spring,
so hungry and so keen
to crawl along the leaves
and feast on something green.

Every spring, millions of caterpillars hatch out of eggs in oak trees to feed on the leaves. There are small green smooth-skinned inchworms, underwing caterpillars that look like tree bark, and many other kinds. Spongy moth caterpillars are pests that can destroy trees, but other caterpillars do not cause serious damage. Some will grow up to become moths and butterflies. Lots will become someone's dinner.

Just ask a chickadee . . .

Chickadee

This is my tree.
I know exactly
where and when
to find the finest pick
of tasty caterpillars
for each and every chick.

Chickadees are among many birds that visit oaks trees to feed on caterpillars. They need to catch a lot of caterpillars, not just for themselves but also for their chicks. Chickadees can lay as many as thirteen eggs. In the sixteen days after their eggs hatch, the parents will need to feed the chicks six thousand to nine thousand caterpillars. When the babies leave the nest, their mom and dad will still bring them food for another two or three weeks. If you want to see chickadees in the spring, there's a good chance you can find them searching for a good meal in their favorite oaks.

Also searching for its next meal is . . .

Orb Weaver Spider

This is my tree,
a perfect place
to spin a web,
supersized and strong,
then wait beside its perfect edge
till dinner comes along.

Birds are not the only insect eaters that hang out in oak trees. Many spiders do too. Orb weavers are known for their circular webs. The lichen orb weaver is one of the largest of its kind, and it can spin a web that is 8 feet (2.4 m) wide. It may sit on a leaf next to its huge web to catch insects, especially gnats, mosquitoes, and flies. If you see an orb weaver in an oak tree, don't be scared. It only wants to bite pesky bugs, not you.

Cicada

This is my tree.
For years I've lived here underground.
I'll crawl out this warm night,
to climb the trunk and shed my skin,
to pause . . . and
then take flight.

Cicadas spend much of their lives underground. But these large bugs start life higher up. Males sing buzzy songs in the treetops to attract females. Females cut slits in twigs and lay their eggs inside. When the eggs hatch, the baby cicadas fall down and burrow in the soil. Some species live underground for as long as seventeen years. Finally, they dig out and climb back up the tree where they molt. Their small wings expand and their bodies harden. Then it's time to fly and sing more buzzy songs or lay more eggs in a favorite tree, which is often an oak.

Who else is singing in the treetops?

Katydid

This is my tree.
In the canopy
this evening,
in the high summer weather,
I'll be singing with my wings,
"It's me! Let's get together!"

Oaks are full of many insect singers. Cicadas are mostly daytime singers. Katydids chorus at night. They are usually green to blend in with the leaves, and they spend their lives in the treetops. From midsummer to autumn, males call to females by scraping part of one front wing against the other. Females choose mates that sing the loudest. Because they live so high up, you probably won't see katydids—but on warm nights you may hear them sing their famous song: "Katy did, Katy didn't."

Big Brown Bat

This is my tree.
A cozy hollow
in the trunk
for daily occupying
provides an easy exit
for all my nighttime flying.

Healthy oak trees can have holes or hollows that make great homes for many different animals. Besides birds, insects, and spiders, mammals may also live in these holes. Among them are various species of bats. Big brown bats are nocturnal. From spring through early fall, they fly out at twilight to find bugs to eat. When the weather turns cold, some types of bats hibernate. Oak hollows provide a warm and safe space for a long winter's nap.

Also keeping safe is a . . .

Screech Owl

This is my tree.
Behind the leaves
against the bark,
I am very hard to see.
Even sharp-eyed hunters
have trouble finding me.

Like most bats, nearly all owls are nocturnal. They rest during the day and hunt at night. Resting gives them energy for their nighttime hunting, but it can also be dangerous, especially for little screech owls. When they are asleep, hawks and other birds of prey may hunt them. How do these owls hide from their enemies? They use camouflage—they blend in with their surroundings so that they are hard to see. Screech owls blend in perfectly with oak bark. They may hide in a tree hollow, or they may sit still on a branch against the trunk. Screech owls are so good at hiding that you're probably more likely to hear their spooky cries than to see them.

Springtail

This is my tree,
though I don't dwell in
the branches
but in litter far below.
I dine on mold and mildew.
I'm a creature you may not know.

Leaf litter is made up of fallen leaves and other plant material, and it's good stuff. It feeds the soil and keeps it moist and free of weeds. It also makes a good hiding place for many animals. And, for some creatures, it provides a good meal. Springtails are buglike, but they have soft bodies and no wings, and unlike true insects, they don't have outside mouthparts. They eat decaying plants, mold, mildew, and pollen. Then they poop out good fertilizer. So leave the fallen leaves under the trees. The oaks and the springtails will thank you!

Blue Jay and Squirrel

Blue Jay: This is my tree.

Squirrel: This is my tree.

Blue Jay: There are acorns.

Squirrel: Many acorns.

Blue Jay: On the branches.

Squirrel: On the ground.

Blue Jay: Some to eat now.

Squirrel: Some to store.

Blue Jay: Time to gather.

Squirrel: Time to bury.

Blue Jay: Get those acorns!

Squirrel: Then get more!

When you think of oak trees, you probably think of acorns. Each acorn is a nut that contains a nutritious seed. Lots of animals eat acorns. Some gobble them up right away. But jays and squirrels will store some in the ground. Later, these critters will dig up many of these nuts to eat. But they won't dig up all of them, and the acorns that stay buried can grow into new oaks. So now when you think of acorns and oaks, you can also think about the jays and squirrels that planted them.

Black Bear

This is my tree.
When I need to eat,
scratch, play
or when I know it's time
to get away from danger,
it's excellent to climb.

Black bears eat all kinds of food. In autumn, acorns make up a big part of their diet, and they will climb oaks to get them. Black bears will also climb trees to protect themselves and their cubs from predators such as wolves, mountain lions, coyotes, grizzly bears, and humans. Even very young cubs are great climbers, and they often enjoy wrestling in the treetops. Bears also like to rub against oaks and other trees to scratch an itch, to get rid of ticks, or to say, “Hey, it’s me” to other bears. They will claw and bite tree bark as well. If you spot these marks, you’ll know that bears have been visiting.

Crows

This is our tree.
We think it's grand
to share a roost
at night or in a storm.
Side by side we huddle close
to keep us safe and warm.

Some birds live alone. Crows like company. On fall and winter evenings, these birds flock together for warmth and protection. Hundreds or thousands of crows may share one roost. Oak trees make particularly good roosts because they are so tall that few predators can reach the treetops. But great horned owls can. These large nocturnal hunters may threaten sleeping crows. But for the crows, there is safety in numbers. Before dawn, the birds greet one another noisily until it's time to fly off and eat. If you live near a crow roost, you may never need an alarm clock.

People

This is my tree.
I love its shade
in summertime,
its color in the fall.
When the leaves return each spring,
I love it most of all.

Oak trees do so much for many creatures, including humans. They absorb chemicals that pollute our water. They store carbon dioxide and release oxygen, which means they help reduce gases that lead to global warming. Their leaves also cool the air by providing shade. And they are beautiful. In autumn, many people become leaf peepers. They flock to places where the trees turn rich red, yellow, and orange. In spring, when the leaves begin to appear, everyone can say, “Glad you’re back!”

Oak Tree

Whose tree am I?
I am yours.
I am mine,
standing tall
in sunlight, snow
and windy weather.

Whose tree am I?
I protect and I nourish
my guests. See how we flourish
when we form a community,
when we live in unity
together!

The Oak Tree Life Cycle

An oak tree starts life as a seed. That seed is inside a tough shell, forming a nut called an acorn. Even though an oak tree can produce many acorns, only a few will become trees.

If an acorn falls (or is buried) in a place with good soil, the acorn will split and send down roots. Then it grows a shoot above the ground. The shoot will sprout small leaves, becoming a seedling. As it grows and makes more leaves, the seedling will also need sunlight for energy. It will continue to grow leaves and a thin trunk, becoming a sapling. Its roots will grow quickly to anchor the tree in the ground and take in water. But it will be many years before it is a fully grown oak. Depending on what type of oak it is, it may become nearly 200 feet (60 m) tall!

When it is 20 to 50 years old, an oak will start to produce acorns—usually around two thousand each year, but on some years as many as ten thousand. It will produce the most acorns between 80 and 120 years of age. But many oaks can live a lot longer than that. Some even live to be 1,000 years or more.

From a tiny seed to a huge ancient tree—that's a mighty oak indeed!

SAPLING
Trunk

How to Recognize an Oak Tree

There may be as many as six hundred species of oak trees found around the world, with ninety of those in the United States. Most oaks are tall with a wide spread of branches and leaves. Their bark is dark and hard and has ridges. Some oaks have smooth, oval leaves. But many are known for their distinctive lobed leaves. All of them produce acorns.

The tree in this book is the white oak, the most common oak species in America. Its leaves are long with rounded lobes.

The red oak is another common species. Its leaves have pointed lobes with bristles at the tips. Because it is fast-growing, the red oak is often planted in city parks and gardens. Both white and red oak leaves change color in the fall to beautiful shades of red.

Why We Need Oaks

Some animals and plants are so important that without them, whole habitats might disappear. These animals and plants are called keystone species. A keystone is the stone at the center of an arch that holds all the other pieces together. A keystone species holds an ecosystem together. Oak trees are keystone species. In North America, oaks are our most important native tree. They offer food, shelter, and places to nest and rest for thousands of animal species. They clean the air and improve the soil. They take in water and help prevent flooding.

But unfortunately, in many places, oaks are disappearing. A major cause of this loss is humans cutting down forests to use the land for farming and buildings. Other causes are pests, disease, and climate change. What can we do to help? We can grow and plant oaks in our neighborhoods. We can make sure they get enough water and good soil. We can check and treat them for disease and pests. We can adopt oaks through many local parks, gardens, and conservancies that will care for them. You can learn how to plant and care for an oak through the National Wildlife Federation (https://www.nwf.org/Magazines/National-Wildlife/2024/Fall/Gardening/Planting-Oak-Trees) and other organizations.

Mighty oaks really can grow from little acorns—especially with our help!

Selected Bibliography

Acton, Jules. *Oaklore: Adventures in a World of Extraordinary Trees*. Greystone Books, 2024.

"Benefits of Oaks." Introduction to Oak Ecology. Accessed June 9, 2025. https://naparcd.org/wp-content/uploads/2017/10/1-Introduction-to-Oak-Ecology.pdf.

Bugman. "Giant Lichen Orbweaver Spider: Anatomy, Behavior, and Habitat Explained." What'sThatBug.com. Accessed June 9, 2025. https://www.whatsthatbug.com/giant-lichen-orbweaver-essential-guide-for-spider-enthusiasts.

Cabrera, Kim A. "Black Bear Marking Trees." Bear Tracker. Updated March 18, 2018. https://www.bear-tracker.com/blackbearscentmarkingttrees.html.

Cicada Mania. Accessed June 9, 2025. https://www.cicadamania.com.

Finch, Katie. "Oaks and Jays." Audubon Community Nature Center, September 26, 2022. https://auduboncnc.org/oaks-and-jays.

Hipp, Andrew L., Paul S. Manos, and Jeannine Cavender-Bares. "How Oak Trees Evolved to Rule the Forests of the Northern Hemisphere." *Scientific American*, August 1, 2020. https://www.scientificamerican.com/article/how-oak-trees-evolved-to-rule-the-forests-of-the-northern-hemisphere.

Jacobs, Steve. "Springtails." PennState Extension. Updated June 19, 2023. https://extension.psu.edu/springtails.

Mahr, Susan. "Katydids." Wisconsin Horticulture. Accessed June 9, 2025. https://hort.extension.wisc.edu/articles/katydids.

Maltbee, Kirk. "What Animals Live in an Oak Tree?" Sciencing. Updated March 24, 2022. https://www.sciencing.com/what-animals-live-in-an-oak-tree-13428851.

Mannio, Cam. "Nourish Nature Around You: Plant an Oak!" Natural Areas Notebook, March 21, 2022. https://oaklandnaturalareas.com/tag/black-capped-chickadee.

McGowan, Kevin J. "Frequently Asked Questions About Crows." Cornell Lab of Ornithology. Updated November 9, 2010. https://www.birds.cornell.edu/crows/crowfaq.htm.

"Oaks Life Cycle Parts of Oak Tree Activities." Montessori Nature, February 28, 2025. https://printables.montessorinature.com/oak-tree-life-cycle-parts-of-printable.

Roach, Margaret. "Why You Should Plant Oaks." *New York Times*, March 31, 2021. https://www.nytimes.com/2021/03/31/realestate/oak-trees-why-you-should-plant.html.

"Roosts in Trees." Bat Conservation Trust. Accessed June 9, 2025. https://www.bats.org.uk/about-bats/where-do-bats-live/bat-roosts/roosts-in-trees.

Tallamy, Douglas W. *The Nature of Oaks: The Rich Ecology of Our Most Essential Native Trees*. Timber, 2021.

Tallamy, Douglas W. "Why We Need More Oaks." *River Cities' Reader*, May 10, 2023. https://www.rcreader.com/commentay/why-we-need-more-oaks.

Todd, Al. "The Nature of Oaks." Cape Conservation Corps, May 10, 2023. https://capeconservationcorps.org/the-nature-of-oaks.

"206-Our Most Essential Trees: The Nature of Oaks, with Doug Tallamy." *The Joe Gardener Show*. Podcast, April 29, 2021. https://joegardener.com/podcast/nature-oaks-doug-tallamy.